HEROINE

Poems by

Sean Andrew Heaney

Thanks to Christopher Kaufman Ilstrup and Stephanie Tuxill at Vermont Community Foundation. In Newport, VT the staff of the Goodrich Memorial Library, Jeannie Pray at Passupsic Savings, Denise Piette and staff at The Front Desk, the Whipple Studio and Christian Kerner.

"Joy and sorrow are one taste. Sorrow can be so deep that it becomes joyful."

-Allen Ginsberg

This book is dedicated
to
Claire Clube, poet and artist of life, asleep in God
and
Brigit Pegeen Kelly
Who thrice gave me the good word

Printed in the United States of America

LIBRARY OF CONGRESS
CATALOGING-IN-PUBLICATION DATA

Heaney, Sean A..
Herione / Sean Andrew Heaney

ISBN 9781936711444

10 9 8 7 6 5 4 3 2 1

Railroad Street Press
394 Railroad St., Ste 2
St. Johnsbury, VT 05819

Table of Contents

The Curse

I stirred a handful of burnt hair
In a glass of water for you:
To not eating, to not sleeping,
To not drinking, to not singing.
To turn your youth into sadness.
To make your sugar tasteless.
To be at odds with your young husband
                              in the night.

As your golden hair turns
To ashen gray
So your young days will
Drift into winter.
To go blind, to fall deaf—
To dry up like grass
And to pass away like breath   .   .   .

She, Herself

after Lucie

Water drops on the lens like the mote of detached
Retina, ice spreads out to the edge like a branch's

Burden. The shutter won't quite close.
In the finder I see the woman halved

In a black moon cup. At the base of the wet
Wickets of a thorn tree, she reaches and lifts
With the tips of her fingers the dark heart

Of an empty bird's nest from the mesh of

Wound sprays. And she has it whole--
Coarse filament of horse hair, a blue chip
Of bloodstained shell, tuft of feather and dun
Of crumbling wattle, all spun once

In a lifting skirt of birds.
Just for the sake of having it she will
Take it home to dry under the stove
And let the mites and parasites out.

And the mist is agent between ground
And sky that rises to wash our hands
And faces and who knows what ghosts
Of us are given up to these? Or

Who she is, goes with me.

Her Leaving

Her ankles were turning blue,
kicking in the cold running water.
But the rest of her skin was as white
as her lace undergarment tented on
a berrybush to dry.
Singing softly to herself,
amused and arrayed in the sun,
She twirled a toe to swirl the pool
and spoil her reflection.
Turning like a cautious doe at my approach,
admitting no immodest touch,
She suffered gladly my reproach
and drawing herself up,
whispered a parable to me
not in words, but in sounds,
with a voice like water over
rocks or the wind knocking
acorns to the ground.
I would not let her spell the stories
end on my eyelids with her fingertips.
I splashed in the pool at her knees
at the flash of spotted feeding fish.
Withdrawing my wrist, I offered her a fistful
of black pearly spawn and the scales
shining on my wet fingers:
Smiling down and catching me in the sunlit slant
of her gaze, I watched her eyes freeze and crack
into blue crystal, and spreading out and sliding
under me, she became the water in the stream
with no need of my gift or useless dream.

Her Wedding

The groom stood apart with ashes on his clothes
while the high white bride flowed down the aisle
trailing maids and myrtle in her train and dark hair.
O my beloved, my Jewess, my intended...

I am the dishonored guest, knocking the pew and sweating
through my suit, counting the relentless measured steps
of her bare feet and the petals falling from the white flower
tacked to her brownred nails.

So walk in your shower of coins and wheat
breathing babies breath,
I paid the girls who guard your veil
my last penny of tribute for wicks and oil
to trace with my lamp the last gleam of your outline
on the warm and twisted sheets.

I hold my peace, walking on the glasses broken
for good luck, thumbing the slit and crack
of the flat black stone hidden in the palm.
Your Father has bled thorn and vine,
mingling grapes and berries to make a wine
to set my teeth on edge.

She hates to see me drink.
I grit and steel myself to drain
the cracked cup down to the last cloves and dregs.
I walk alone to cast this ring of bone and semi-precious
stone, my evil eye, in the ocean.

Her Keening

for Nuala O'Faolain

Please give no thought to flowers.
Buy a drink for the sundered couple instead.
I don't know how many times I brought him water,
or rolled him over in my Mum's clean bed.
The last time he came to me his whole body
trembled, then he died in my arms like a child.
This time I've laid him out proper, but that's
the last time that we shared a bed. Don't think
me hard for leaving him then, wasn't it him
put these webs around my eyes, the kind that mad
spiders spin? While I was out working he'd be gone
chasing chippies or soaking in up with the boys.
It's lovely quiet now, I'm feeling blessed.
It was always the girl floating in the glass that he
loved best. If you'd heard him sing and whisper things
to her, you'd know it was true. Imagine me playing
second fiddle to my babies bottle! He was a deep dreamer
and a noontime sleeper in a condition, and me always up
with the birds. "Moonface," old poetmouth would call me,
for always looming over him...But shed no tears for me,
that's the only legacy he left me. And save your prayers,
thank you, I mistrust soft words thanks to him. It's the
priest and the poet I've learned to dread. If I see one coming
I'll pull my shawl over my shoulders, to cover him too, to keep
those fiery coals off my head.

The Firebrand

Up there the turning of the year
was Winter just beginning. Canadian coldfronts
barrelled down like old freights across the Georgia
high bridge, over the crackle on the lake of ice fisherman's
fires; a keen sting of crystals in the North wind
chasing the flying figures of skaters home to watch
the ragged flakes, like a million riderless white
ponies, dash against the picture window pane.

My Father swung the kerosene stove like a lantern
to rest in the center of the room, priming then lighting
its metallic gasp and hiss into fuelled breath of fire.
It cast a many patterned wheel on the ceiling,
and the parents retreated to the shadows, Mother's voice
speaking low to him of an old story and him saying
nothing, tilting back with a bottle of Bally, tracing
the labels three connected rings of "Goodness, Body
and Purity."

O Fire Wheel, heavy planet, burning flower
Your radiant circumference is a child's idea of Heaven,
star sphere, showing more than stained glass or television
The waking infant in the crib cries to see you
there. Brothers and sisters on the floor with singing
fingers make shadow animals; the bull, the bird, the hare
move in a ring at the rim of your Zodiac glow. They rise
and grow to giant size over our St. Vitus dance under
your never sleeping eye in the heat of made up music
'til one of us let go the grasp . . .   *ashes, ashes*
we all fall down.

Now Winter is a white room, lit by a single candle flame.
Three siblings are asleep in God.
I dip a waxed nail over the tip of the twisted taper
and snuff the wick with a burnt fingerprint.
In darkness under flickering lids the sun that
is always with me, leaves me, and rises again
on the wall.

A Pox On This House

This house was long ago divided & set against itself.
Everyone was sent out alone, turned upon their own ways.
The toys are in the attic & spiders spin the fallen moths.
Grapes no longer grow over the walls
The arbor is an empty frame.
The elderberries haven't come back as they once did,
There is a dead rat in the ceramic wine vat in the cellar.
The gardens are choked & growing over, climbing
milkweed & sumac trees are coming in to claim the fields.
The family has been poisoned long and slow, something
leaching underground into the water in the well.
Pentagram nailed on the shed wall spins a curse
to the four corners of the farm.
The first woman of this house, a witch, Anna,
became an anathema when the village learned of her
practices & strange spells; children & livestock fallen ill.
Driven from the land, she put her hand over this place.
When the rabble came with sticks & torches
she drove the horse-drawn cart while the old man
stood in the back of the wagon & held the mob
off her with spit, oaths, & a pitchfork.
With the reins in one hand she mumbled incantations
to the air, touched a black crucifix between her tits
& fingered a wreath of human hair, on the way back
over the mountain where she came from with signs
following.

EQUITATION

For my father, Joseph P. Heaney

From My Father on My Birthday

"With many happy
Returns of the day.
Remember:

There exist only
Three beings worthy of your
Utmost respect: the Priest,

the Soldier, and
the Poet. To Know, To Kill,
To Create.

Works of great poets
Have never yet been read by
Most of mankind, for

Only great poets
Can read them. As for money,
Don't worry about it.

For many years
I was overseer of snow
storms and rain storms,

Guardian of hay fields, horses
And children, did my duty
Faithfully though

I never received
A cent for it."

Chief Joseph

Chief was "a Palouse horse"
or Appaloosa
White & mottle coated
Special breed of the Nez Perce
Good stock for racing, the hunt
or battle. He was every inch
my father's horse.

His favorite in our stable.
Misty was the Fair Lady,
Loner the brooding stud &
Blaze the gifted grouch.
He named him Chief Joseph.
Something in the horse's face,
his bearing, a quiet dignity
recalled the leader of that tribe:
(Photograph, Montana Historical Society.)

Soon after settling our New Hampshire farm,
he mounted him for a trail ride along
abandoned logging roads,
wound like ferns through the forest
pointing off in all directions
some that circled back upon
themselves leading nowhere at all.

He was gone too long – night overtook him.
When the woods become a shadowland
the eyes play tricks; all paths loom
as dark possibilities.

11

That is when the rider gives himself
over to horse sense, leans forward on the
mane speaks low to the animal's
second sight, trusts him
to lead him back to the barn.

We were waiting on them
when the Centaur came
up the lane to rejoin
the herd, its head bobs & nods in
the grain barrel.

How many seasons had he when my father told me,
"I have to have Chief put down.
He's gone blind with age and a malady
peculiar to the breed. It's not a pretty thing
to see."

I thought of his namesake's final supplication
the tribe run off, the herd collared,
Chief Joseph bound and snowblind
at the frozen borderline.

In Heat

I awoke in summer from a dream
Sweating the dew point, mist blown on my face
through the sifting screen, heat lightening shorts
the radio's static air.
Restless turning on sheets of institutional blue;
She is only night shade, clocks tick of loss,
my heart's insistent murmur . . . or now the clop
of shod hooves on wet pavement.

The neighbor's mare from down below is in heat.
She has untethered herself, nosing the smells
in a foaming sweat on the humid night air that
off & on relieves itself in rain.
A mixed breed buckskin, she comes trotting blonde
in the darkness to where our geldings nod by the gate.

She is unbridled; my Father in his bathrobe from his
bed & cigar smoke tries to slip one on her head.
She has awakened something in them, they nip and jostle
each other to get at her, not a stud among them but none
resigned to skittish teaser; There is a flash of teeth,
a wheeze & whinny, the spook in a blueblack eye
when she breaks his grip, clears the stonewall
on a stride.

She cut through the herd like a wild white streak
I am in the middle with a coil of rope.
Our horses are rearing up & dancing around her until they
freeze in the headlights of the neighbors truck & the slow
approach of the shadow figures of her owner & his son
coming to take her saying, "Easy girl, easy," as they lead her
back in a borrowed halter.

13

My Father tells them not to be cavalier about the dangers
of a loose horse. They are silent & return without thanks.
But the night is coming when we will awaken to a winter sky on fire
from their barn burning from neglect, & see that mare bolting
the flame & heat across the snowfield.

Baby Spinaway

That horse was all of love
my father ever gave to me.

I called her Baby Spinaway:
and how he came to *hate* her.

She would not let herself be broken.
"I should have busted her when she was a filly," he said.

She was so fast, she was almost of the air
with no saddle on her back.

"That mare is useless to a man.
you get on her and stay on her a few minutes
then end up on your head and what does it prove?"

He still tried;
She returned with one black boot dangling from the stirrup
head up high and riderless, saddle uncinched and askew.

She was watch-eyed; I don't know where that word comes from,
only that her eyes were like sky and powder blue.
They say I spoiled her even more –
that much is true.

I'd braid her mane with ribbon and shine her flanks with
mint oil so you could smell her coming sweet on the wind.

I wasn't sad when my Dad died.
He'd gotten meaner with age, couldn't ride anymore.

He didn't seem sad, either.
On his deathbed he told me:

"I buried your mother after you were born:
now you'll bury me."

No one gave me away when I was wed:
a nice guy, I didn't marry my father.

He doesn't argue and does what I say: "Bring Baby hay, grain and water,"
he wouldn't say no, and he just does it like a dutiful groom.
When I was late with child I hated being away from her.
I'd stand by the gate and talk to her, but it wasn't like it was before.

I brought her green apples which she snapped and chewed
and dropped a frappe of white slather down my thigh.

At night I'd lie awake feeling sick
and heavy with the kicks in my side.

My husband wanted a son; now he'll never have one.
I told him when our daughter was born after nine hours labor:

"No more."
I know it can't be done, but I'd
always have Baby stay the same--

Never change for anything or anyone.
To always stand alone, never knocked up

to foal, be broken in or used for show.
Then I could say, "I kept her the better part of me."

I'd have this, my mare, my woman's wish, and
let them all tell me I'm crazy.

The Quarry

I

Here where four fields meet, there is the common
ground of the town's first cemetery, seeded with
it's founding families. This is the way you must go
to walk on turned furrows to a stand of trees to swim
this summer in the granite quarry, whose yield grows
here perennially, life's labor and strife summed up
with hammered dates and a carved quatrain, Death
Angel presiding; "So Jesus slept, God's dying Son,
passed through the grave and blessed the bed; Rest here,
dear one, 'til from his throne the morning breaks to
pierce the shade. . ." Walking away from my father's
house the light burned stripes on my shoulder blades,
the drudge pulls the plow 'til he strikes rock, and the
snake writhes around the sun in the talons of the hawk.

II

Is this pool of memory spring or stream fed?
The journeymen long forgotten, the quarry cannot be sounded
in fathoms, where the rock was chiseled and blasted
Water was struck, covered scree and filled the chasms
and rose up to receive rain and gather runoff.
Dive from a crag into dark water through the sun's
reflective rash, plumb the depths where no one can touch you,
past terraced slabs, black with decomposing leaves, down
cold stone stairs to brush the smooth kiss of broken
statuary where one ray penetrates like a silver silken thread.
But for craving air and light you could hang suspended
forever in cool museum...So flex back up to stroke
in the foam wake, and in the wash of your vision find
faces in the rock and catch the bodies dancing on the
rippled surface of the water.

III

I am alive in the sun on the steps of this flooded
unfinished temple, hearing the hummingbird by my ear.
I watch our myths unfold in moving diamond patterns
and hourglasses cast on the walls from the water's reflection.
Leaning back on the soft matted grass on the wet stone,
I let a dragonfly land on a sun bleached page of Li Po
The light through it's purple wing puts color on the leaf.
Turning over, I see her in profile, climbing from her bath,
feeding seeds to tiny fish gathered at the lip of the white ledge.
She picks up a pine cone and a piece of smoothed glass rolls
in her palm like a drop of molten gold that makes my eyes ache.
Dreams abide beneath this rock, her leaning over me while the
weave of branches behind her head holds the skies great opera;
Music for voices and woodwind.

IV

We loved to turn our faces to the rain . . .
When we awoke it was already falling
The clouds were not ominous when they opened,
the water softened on the wind and we saw circles
within circles on the smoked glass surface,
like skipping stones or acorns dropping in a pool
from the overhanging bough. It was then I felt chill,
the wing fell over me, the blue heron, flapping down
like a transformed Deity, shadow spanning both banks;
A woman changed by jealousy passing strange.
Fear of being followed come as sudden as this shower,
I froze while she watched me from the bracken
and felt the lash on my cheek when the bird flew away . . .
Speech stolen, no tongue to tell of this, let her divine
an answer from the sound of falling water
drops.

Ashes of Roses

Rose Window/Venus Rising

In the white room   before the sun   she gathers her reflection
in the cup of her hands   from a standing bowl of attar
The pour and splash refreshes her face   petals oil rolls
down her arms skin of milk and cinnamon   drops run to the
ruddy tips of her breasts moistened   fingers touch her temples
The scent of roses fills the air   where there is only the
shaking wetness of her cleansed red hair   She will gather the
curls and strands together   fasten them with a spun gold
clasp   to the cool appraisal of the looking glass
Arms raised about her head   her white shift of linen
slips to the floor   a flower opens slowly
Under the rose   her feet move softly over the rills and
folds of her fallen bedclothes   that smell of aloe
to face the stations and mysteries of the day
She warms herself in the center of the circle of the window
The sun cuts sharp-edged petals of the panes   blown glass
blossom animated by light holds the figure whole within
the wheel   closing her eyes   turning her head from the glare
She is caught and freed as she dreams the world
and covers her wound with her hand and her hair.

Solstice

The theme of the wedding was a seasonal dream
When winter and spring came on the same day.
All morning I watched the reception of wet snow
On budding branches and early bloomers;
By afternoon the snow veiled the pastures
Began to blind the windows, sending wind down
The chimney in the empty stove. Snapped
At last the electric wires, and the house found itself
Again lit by candle power as the drifts climbed the clapboards;
By nightfall the farm was a black and white world.
This freak storm comes of white magick, wise woman,
White like yesterday's flowers and feathers in your hatband,
White like the page that holds your pure words,
White like the lacy hem of your folded dress,
White like your shoulders and thighs and breast,
White like the starched sheets of linen on your bed,
All as white as what we dream together asleep under
The curved spine of the Aphrodite tree laden with snow.

Small Game

The snow has made a white fan
over the mouth of the stream
the water whispers and flutters
under, sleet sculpts slumbering nudes
from the rocks in the riverbed that lie
beneath the tangled arbor of frozen branches,
fused and frozen by ice that hives sunlight,
as it drips and glistens down the bowed curve
to the dark roots of young trees that warp and
weave to hold up the egg blue sky.

Across the white spread a swatch of red fur
pulls a thread to the edge of the glazed hem.
This crystal ice can only hold the tracer of a
foxtail skittering with its meal in its mouth
to the lair the blundering hunter
can't uncover.

At the edge of Coburn Woods
foxfire glows on the high white walls.
Ice cubes melt in a crystal goblet of amber
mead that you hold, resting cushioned in
your dominion.

Red pelt sleek, washed and combed...
there are no dark undercurrents here
you cannot cross over, no sniffing hound let
slip from this pack you can't elude nor heavy tracker
tread you can't outpace by repair to that deep
place of your musky scent and birthmark.

The Three Marys

"You wouldn't know her now if you
passed her on the street," but no
mistaking that crimson mane down
by the crosswalk on Tremont Street.
She looks for all the world like a girl
playing Dress-Up, tottering on the broken
heel of mother's black patent leather shoe.
"Worn out by the pavement, no doubt."

Going with the light and her own
right-of-way, she may stop for window
wishing at the glass nativity in seasonal array;
Green eyes capture the prism color from
the mirror edges of the miniature figurines.
"If she had any shame she'd be sweating like a
whore in church."

Her moment wonder makes brief festival
of our commerce and traffic.
Under the vault the bank clock
ticks off another year; time and the city
in conspiracy keep her from me.
Lady Rose walks off alone in her
camel's hair coat, beneath the single star
of bulbs and wire mesh, strung out netting
the night air before it gets dark and they're
turned on. "Are we shopping or stalking?"

Cold condense the conversation
like the breath of smoke and resolutions:
They blow along the thoroughfare going

the way of all our good intentions.
"She'll get hers in the next life;
Too bad we have to wait so long."

North Shore/Cape & the Islands

Eventide

Feel the weight of darkness falling wet.
Mist swells the planks of the deck

Of *The Bachelor's Delight,* tidal rip giving up
Blues on my watch where freighters rest & rust

By Grave's Light, mates asleep
In bunks in the cabin while saltwater warps

Docks, rots fishnets & curls back
The pages of Melville's great book.

The swells buoy tones of the vesper bells,
The eye of Venus a conspicuous matchlight

On the chapel-gray tower of Our Lady
Of Good Voyage. I could see her coming caped

In fog, the ballad-seller in sailor's dress,
Humming snatches of garlands, catches

& slipsongs. The drone & whine
Of the pressed bladder of bagpipes played

Amazing Grace (how sweet the sound)
Into a spinning reel as she showed me the star

Drawn on her palm & the anchor tattooed
On her heel. I saw the ships in the sunken

Light of her mooncussing eyes; I said
You are the siren that lures vessels

To keelsplitting wrecks. She said:
I am the song you can't forget,

The lucky one, the thresher in your net.

Strange Cargo

We'll give a miss to the dreary wake of Allston bookstores loaded stalls
and biers; warmth in December is rare. We'll drive clear to Winegarsheek
and Singing Beach, impulse trip to Gloucester.

Bootheel halfmoons dance in the sandpainting of brown swirls and black
grain. Gulls leave a trail of broken crosses when they walk upon it.

Mixed signals flare conversation. Women are prayer and poison, work is
penance and confession. Frail yeomen pace the bridge beneath the ancient
wheelman in his frozen Mac. We grip the rail and sight the cedar leaf of
gold,
rolled in the wave crest, the promise I recited to you from memory.

Salted air keens appetite. I must be fed.
In the Portuguese cafe I sit with my back against the wall like a gangster.
Everyone is smoking here. It is broken into beams through slats of
shuttered
light onto checkered tablecloths. You'll take only beer, tang of hops to
spice and loosen the tongue. You dip a crust of bread in my plate
when I cut you a piece of seasoned meat.

History is alive in that old man behind you with a wooden cross and
beaded
string floating around his neck, a mumbled Patois Grace over a frugal
meal,
his good eye watering uncontrollably, tears rolling down his face. Yours
are . . .
Variable, cloud and clear by turn. I watch for storm warnings when you
remember California and the rest of America.

Lady Rose and Lady Bernadette are listing on plum wine water mingled

with oil. Softshell crabs litter the wet brick walkway. Olson sits oppressive
as the church on the hill, we'll clock each other yet with his leviathan
Maximus.

The day has turned gray as Sterling's beard, all the way home it is our
fathers, our fathers, and we the legacy, gone all quiet now we don't even
play the radio. Dark along the Charles black channels until we see the
city's neat geometry by the river. The Hancock tower has thrown ten
thousand mirrors against the sky, cloud silo takes Winter's temperature,
reflects back on us in a shimmer of light. Some nights it all connects and
glows; Disperses darkness revealing you to me and shows us how
we live like this.

The Seer

Grammy Proctor was born with a caul;
Hood of flesh and blood, loose and membranous,
Snipped and lifted away after birth.

Midwife hags would swab and save them
In burlap bags and hawk them to sailors on the docks of
Salem, rank charm for a safe voyage.

Those born of this ordeal are said
To be touched; Given the mixed blessing
Of prophecy.

Burden of the uncanny within
The quotidian. Lying awake all night
With all those other lives in mind.

Drawn awake to a spot in the backyard
Under the elm branch shadow to say,
"It happened here," and there was where the former
Lady of the House had hanged herself.

Gram grew into a good Christian woman.
The crucifix was the poppet with the pin
In it. Cunning folk never used the gift for gain
Or profit, talked of it in roundabout, made a game
Of what was in the cards or what the leaves spelled
In the swirl at the bottom of the teacup.

But when the boy from downstreet disappeared,
She knew. She saw the before, the during and the after
In particular order: The man escaped from Danvers

Appeared at the child's sand pile and said, "I Am
Jesus Christ." Abduction, asphyxiation...body removed
To a cold place --- pale fetal form of the blond boy
soon found in the ice house.

After that she went all quiet,
Despaired of ever seeing the good again:
"There is a sign on me," she told mother and auntie.
One night she stood up abruptly, crossed herself, said;
"I am going to sleep," pitched forward and was
Dead before she hit the floor.

Down The Cape

At Race point the sun went down on fire
all boats burning, lost armada, last light
tinned on the water, pounded leaf from
the goldsmith's hammer tempered on the
heavy blue metal of the sea.

Twilight makes us in half light
on the jettie's odd shaped rocks
(pretend you lost a contact lens)
past Hopper's lighthouse to the tidal flats,
where every bird comes to drift like snow
the rushes ravel out sweetflag, goldenrod and
lavender thrift by the guiding glow of cigarettes.

Tossing waves too full of sound and foam
drop their mail of shells, stones and starfish
on the bar, cream and moan and swirl into
everlasting mother-of-pearl.
On the arm's pith and marrow we watch
the polished yacht's white sail go rose,
cut and turn into black and blue.

At last your voice calling from the island
on the waterbottom cable, like Lady Day,
Bird with strings and pennant races on public radio;
Provincetown in evening dress of chimes, lanterns
and foreign tourists; bars full and overflowing.

Summer Ferry To Martha's Vineyard

Half-seven miles off the southeast coast, and glad to be, the boat
bulls its way with braying horn on the torn foil sea, lording it over
smaller crafts just past the Gothic horror of the Kennedy compound.
I thought of the death of Irish kings, and the pull of the tides to a
Vineyard Haven in the county of Dukes, and the frail barque of the first
white men to lay eyes on it, "This island is sound, and hath no danger
upon it."
Then they named them for daughter and Queen. My thoughts
became narcotic, lost in some heroic-epic, read once and half
remembered, 'til my eyes caught a cloudshape that took up half the sky,
of a white bird with a woman's head, come on the wing to give gracious
escort, the whole shadow of Heaven, Anna from the very skies, or Maya's
dance of The Seagull, like a white gardenia floating in a silver bowl.
Better men have bent every arrow in the quiver for such a sight outside of
sleep, become as children picked up in her beak and dropped to die on
the beach amongst the splintered whalebone.

The Elizabeth Islands

We are borne and baptized when the breakers
wash our feet, we immerse in clear water,
swimming mid-day along the cove
where Maushope changed his children to fishes.
Sidestroke on the ribs of sand, bubbling to burst
to the surface, cruise in the curve of a wave
head still sounding shell hiss soft
white noise of the surf's permissive kiss.

Flying in our element between earth and air
confirmed sighting of your breed among the
waterbirds come to rest on this strip of sand.
Free of land persuasions, sleek and coweled
we nest and feed on broken bread, eggs-in-the-grass;
champagne grapes caught between teeth and tongue
juice runs sharp on cracked lips, salt's chalk cakes
your lashes and dries on your breastbone in the sun.

Gulls and terns bobbing on thermals,
from the white cliff I'd test my span
across the sound to Elizabeth's Island,
her dense green thick with flowers, sweet
springs; You are asleep, one knee up,
head turned in.

Bed and Board

Last words to me when we were alone:
"Susan is my best friend. Be nice
To her, she's been depressed."
Now we're lost; no one says anything
For fear of the wrong thing: Just us three,
Crowded in the car, wrapt in thoughts contrary.

Something haunted about the island
Driving back at night on the wrong road
That is dark and knotted, an oak's root.
We missed a sign and can't steer by the stars
Behind the low cloud cover.

Feeling our way we find the house where
Two cats, jet black, greet us on the wet grass.
The dog has his back up by the pile of logs
Cut and stacked for the lady-of-the-house.

Something funny in the stair's creak,
The way we walk in quiet deference
To the hundred years memories of other
Boarder's stories in these rooms,
Former farm, now guest house.

Something beastly in our fatigue
That puts hooks and catches in conversation
A wash of sand, soap slivers and spiders
In the shower drain; portents heavy
In the air like the blue haze of our cigarettes
Hanging in our room: and you don't smoke.

Susan has gone out fearless to sleep
In the field, to leave us to silent argument,
Where she'll dream of Western deserts and
The canyons of her Manhattan. We can't fight it;
Tonight we bundle cold spine to cold spine
Drifting off I have the hot bath of memory
For who came before or this new familiar
With a twist. Oceana Materna, statuesque
Voluptuary, rocking and rolling over me,
As I slip back to she who penned my story.

Lands End Light

I have good eyes.
I have kept my vigil. While the sun is out
                    I do my reckoning
by shadows and the motion of the sea, I have kept
the sweep of my gaze hard along the horizon, squinting
at what might lie beyond it. I wouldn't see a body
burning on the beach or on my ship if it came in
at my feet. So my vision finds distraction
                    in the idling of three girls along the shore,
the Sisters of Nauset pose as Graces stripped
to the waist, while my mind makes a war of the nesting
terns that bring the pitch of their attack in singing.

                    *

The beach at night is a stranger scene,
to walk against a curve of lights along the cove
to where the girl dropped her mirror
beneath a rose moon enclosed within a silver ring.
                    Tonight she will show me everything;
drawing all the water from the harbor up into Heaven,
pulling back the veil to reveal a sunken
garden blooming in the desert like an open grave.

*

You went into this with your eyes open.
You knew what she was when you married her.
In the morning walk on the way back to town
you say nothing to anyone about what you think
you saw.
         Be thankful for your dry clothes
and the tough soles of the shoes on your feet.
Walk the waterfront streets among foreign women,
cross dressers and fishermen.
            And when the Sisters
of Sappho serve you a pearl on the halfshell
in the raw bar, smile and swallow it, tear the bread
gently and soak the scud of butter off the top of the white
steaming broth.

         Let your eyes rest
on the bird alight outside on the line
as the woman, slick from her shower,
bends down, tying her sandal, shaking water like glass beads
and baubles, drying her hair in the sun. Maybe she'll
give me a ride home . . . I missed my friends.
I am alone and I am not aftraid.

Too Much Sun

August searing the straits of noon burning down a summer's day
at Head-Of-The-Meadow, grit on the slowly peeling skin of bodies
entangled on the sand that crack and wrinkle like old maps as terns
scale the white air. NO SWIMMING: MEDICAL WASTE and the
red tide sucks what wind there is out of the hour. Brit and kelp
roil on the rocks. The eyes sting and the ears ache to swim in it.
I'll find no precious metal buried here and won't ask for arms
to carry it back when I retreat, the sun my enemy, the water's
taunting at last intolerable like the mind's babble. Nothing
for it but the trudge to the private beach on the safe side,
tent pitched on a dune tuft, airless inside by wrapped bedrolls.
No shade but blue sky. You could swim in the clear water here
if the waves were not casting up a sheet and lode of stones from
the bottom to rain down on you if you test it.   She is standing
at the edge. She won't talk to me, a few words to save the day,
a grace note, but no, she hides behind her hair and Ray-Bans.
I'm afraid I don't care who you are, look at me when I talk to you.
She stands mute. I have enough words inside myself for two:
                You must change your wife.

California Suite

I

What is today? No matter .   .   .
Here they fall on one another, uniform,
perfect, suffocating. No different today,
my birthday. Boredom to distraction. Need a mission.
To walk through the valley with no Virgil guide.
Go up the heat shimmering Maricopa highway
as far as the crow flies. A hawk idles,
then spirals down on its prey in the brown
burnt grass: Seems savage enough.
Where water cuts the rock the smell of sulphur
burns air. Matilija curative waters have their
price, and a NO TRESPASSING sign by the reservoir.
I trip on broken beer bottles left by bikers and Whitman
bathers splayed on the rocks; bleeding, cursing .   .   .
Who'll protect us from each other, from ourselves,
is thought enough for one day,
One Hades.

II

Much as anything that brought me here,
A friend back East whose open book and scattered
coin spelled; Fire On The Mountain. Distant travel
was what I wanted. Then that summer Saturday night
Santa Anna witchy wind blew hot breath, we saw sparks tinder
on the rocks to set a whole range ablaze. Soft ember glowing
night of palominos running spooked in fields by trees frosted with
ashes and moonlight. The fire brigade had started it by burning
slash in the forest: "We had to burn it to save it." The wind did the rest.
Bad Nam visions for days as coptors sucked water from the ocean
to drop on the Old Chief's scarred face. The black smoke burned
a red sun Rose in the sky. I drank gin with blood in my eye.
Come this far cross country to burn our way to the sea.

III

The bells of El Camino Real mark the missions set in warm adobe
all along the coast, Spanish Holy names spoken softly underbreath
Scented mayflower surrounding Mary in her bower, lurid, flesh-hung
Christs life-size over dripping votive lighters, mysterious
bi-lingual epistles to Mother Superior. Nights of faith in the
faithless and drinking for our sins have made me fluent in this
language I no longer understand, but for the comfort of it's shroud.
Still to put up a prayer for this ritual violence and the politics
of Ecstasy; one wise sheep knows his Father, the Great Bell-wether.
To be where, for one minute, the palms outreach your spire!
Watch sunset sky drain from tempra blue to pink to no color.
On the docks where bored fishermen sit and face the Orient.
Joy to see one seal bob up, playing free beneath the pier
Curse of recognition at the red and white daredevil hooked in his
head . . . the reach extends even here. His mate washed up on the shore
decapitated by a shark or motor blades. *La dolce vita* in California.
You see the face of your saving grace, her words drowned out by the
water and the wind. You can't even translate the sign language of
innocence. Ingénue. Sad movies.

Shanks Mare

"If wishes were horses, beggars would ride..."
She coined that for me back when we still rode together.
Back when every night was a bucking canter
That combed the dreamfield of her dark hair
Beneath the spilled blood money on the Hunger Moon.

Tall, cinched, astride 'til dawn on high cantle,
How many days from sundust were we when I let
Her drift; lost my mount ground-tied in open country?
Rein in hand became a handful of nothing put the sand
I trampled under foot, unclenching my fingers.

Saddle tramp in hobbling boots
I'll not bargain with a rogue for
A cameo in this horse opera.
I'll live with the notion of my mare
Running free

Not the thought of her roped,
Broken, and put through the paces
By a stranger's steady hand.
This is the spur that goads my flesh
Across the white sand

Between the winds towards a lone star
That studs the sky like another sun
Blinding the eye to no horizon.

Drop A Line

POSTMARK: Santa Monica.
Meet me on the boardwalk at the Mermaid Cafe.
I'll be right here where she left me. I do all
the cliché things: Walk the promenade. Eat cotton
candy. Buy balloons and let them go. Watch
the stars in bars, say "No," to the teenage Mexican
girls who ask me, "Do you want some company?"
and I do but I don't go into the cool of the shadows
under the pier; you don't know what is waiting
there. I go for my pint of bitter and the barlight
to write by, listening to the calliope dirges
from the carousel that send the wooden horses up
and down in an vicious circle. Memory
serves me well as I recall the holidays with two
whom love protects. We are in for some weather
and that never happens here. A black sky storm that
will play Hell on the coast and tear the old lady's shell
and ships in bottles shop right off the end of the dock into
the foam where it belongs. I won't be home by then.
My friends, I send you this; my love, a chart less course,
Something missed.

Arias I Love: Some Women

VALENTIN; Who do *you* identify with?
MOLINA: Oh, the singer. She's the star. I'm always the Heroine.

-Kiss of the Spider Woman

Tell All, Ann Dvorak

Hollywood.
I hate this town. I'd always go my own way.
Nobody could show me, I was on the screen as babe
in my mother's arms before the flickers went West.
My mother was in silents, a Jewish Princess, and
the director was my father, Black Irish McKim.
Then one day he was gone just like that, just like a man.
I was straight out of Hollywood High
and stepped out of the chorus line to slap
Jack Benny's face in MGM's first talkie,
"The Hollywood Review of 1929."
I taught a lot of the girls how to dance
but still lost parts to ham-and-egg hoofers like
Ruby Keeler. Everyone knew I had the best bustle in the biz.
Howard Hughes took me, but I didn't get taken,
just became a star in the original "Scarface," as
Cesca, the gangster's sister, and we played the incest
thing just right. This was Pre-Code. I was
Hawks protégé without lying down. He used me in two
pictures, but never had me, like he lost his
later discovery, Lauren Bacall, to Bogie.
It was like a fighting family, and I hated all
three Warner Brothers, they'd put me in anything
so I went on suspension. "You're not Bette or Cagney,"
they told me, so I married a pretty nice guy
my co-star and a would be director. We went to England
and I made pictures there, but I was in the war before
Pearl, drove an ambulance and wrote home what was coming.
Back in the Industry I'd had my day, a few good bits
here and there, not the good girl or vixen anymore but the drunk
or the shrew. I did okay, married a mad Russian dancer

who beat me, so I gave him the air. When Mum died I went
to the press to search for my father. They found him, the old soak,
in Florida in a seedy old orange grove. He knew all about me,
just didn't care. At least he didn't ask me for money.
For me, with men, the third time was a charm and my public life is over.
I live in Hawaii with my husband, we collect first editions.
I'm happy though I've already got the cancer that will kill
me. I don't complain. Sour grapes was never my dish.

I Tried to Die but Now I Want to Live: Jennifer Jones

The Lady told me, "I can't promise to make you
happy in this life, only in the next."
You see, I think very few people are happy.
They wait all their lives for something to happen to them,
something great and wonderful. They don't know what it is,
but they wait for it. Sometimes it never happens. What they
want is a kind of spirit, the spirit that makes life beautiful.
Always before our eyes is a vision of beauty,
a beauty which we've never seen,
but which makes everything we do see
unbearable.
I think we can see what lies ahead.
I mean, what is going to happen to us.
You know how you feel sad about things sometimes,
about things that have never happened.
Perhaps they are the things that are going to happen to us . . .
Maybe we're here to learn to suffer gracefully,
with faith in what we can't see. Sister,
I have lived many lives on screen and off,
buried three husbands, saw my daughter do away
with herself and I tried suicide three times.
Losing my memory is a blessing; I lost my Oscar.
I live with my son from my first marriage,
the love match, truest, best. He's the image of his father.
Now I act my age, and have learned to like it;
This coming to rest.

Iseult Gonne

I was the young girl dancing in the wind…
In faith I wish I had stayed that way.

Yeats was my mother Maude's true love,
but she had the Cause and her martyr, my father,
McBride: Proud, cruel and a mean drunk.
She didn't have much use
for men, and said, "If there was another way to have children
I'd have done it," but her youthful beauty was gone
while mine was my way into their society
where I learned many things.
Uncle Willie said I was his protégé, and
we traveled in literary and spiritual circles.
When he asked my mother for my hand,
she left it up to me; I think she thought
it was funny. I blushed for him.

He should have just taken me when he had the chance,
Uncle Ezra did: it was lovely, really, though
I closed my eyes. He looked like the Devil himself;
he taught me the romance languages and to never trust a Jew.
He lost interest soon enough, anyway he never had a shilling.
I have to say if I'd married Yeats it would have been
sweet revenge on my Mum, myself the picture of what
she used to be, the muse of all his poetry, now the crone in black.
He finally married a fool but she was clever in craft.
Let her bear him a brood and live in a Tower.
I'm my father's daughter and will only wed the one
who won't take any brass from me and if he is a brute I swear
to God I'll laugh at myself for being just a woman like all the others.

Once I was the young girl dancing in the wind.
I would to God I had died that way.

Tamsen Donner

It is really only me now.
I gave my children away
To the rescue party. Better that way,
That they think I'll stay with their father.
Meet up with them another day if they make it.
My husband is dead in a tent so covered
In snow that it looks like a tomb of Vermont granite.
We are from the East; it never snowed like this.

I talked to him while he lay there dying
Out of his wits, talking of the trip
And all the things we brought with us, treasure
And domestic, that we dropped off the side
One by one:
The brass bedstead, the pianola and then leaning
Over, my cameo made a blue hole in the snow.
We burned every page in the family Bible.
That night the heavy weather buried the oxen in
Their yoke ten feet at least. We heard their braying
On the drift and wind. In the morning
It was still snowing and they were gone under
White boughs bent to breaking. We didn't know
Where we were and we were dying.
The last word he said was "Mother."

It is really only me now.
I started walking towards the ridge, the whole range
Staring me in the face. It is snowing again .   .   .
I know I'm not really going anywhere.
I am mummified, marrow eating bone.
I am animal in the wilderness disappearing

59

In the West of my white oblivion.

Lucy Harker

---Nosfertu

"If a woman pure of heart
Can hold the beast through the night
Until daybreak, dawn will kill him
and the pestilence be ended..."
I know now
What I must do.
My very name means Light.
My husband is now a stranger:
"Who is this woman to me?"
I will cast away my cross and put on
My wedding gown, the dress I wore when
I first died to the woman I might have been.
I will take to my bed and wait for he that comes.
Array my hair just so on the pillow, bare my neck.
Let him bleed myself to whiteness.
Make him stay with me past the hour of his death.
Rise again from the winding sheet.
Science is old men counting the dead
When the wolf is at the door.
I know now
What I must do.
Ride the dark horse to the next town, then the next.
They are already trying to hide from me.
They know what I bring.
I have seen my reflection for the last time.
Now I will live forever.

Sister Juana

Sor Juana de la Cruz
In Spain, I'm known as "The Tenth Muse."
That was said before only of Sappho,
But Time has made an error.
God is my Father, I never knew my own.
My mother is not my mother: my mother is Sophia,
Goddess of Wisdom, not the woman who sold me
to the Court in Mexico, Lady-In-Waiting waylaid
by my priest to a nunnery where he promised I could devote
My life to study. I teach little Sisters to sing songs I write,
I have my poetry, Heaven through my telescope, and my
black obsidian mirror in which I see the past and future.
The worst of it is I am a woman with only books for children.
Men hate me for it, though they laugh at my comedies,
They fear me. "Whenever I hear a woman speak, I hear a viper."
I tried to bring Beauty to thought, not thought to Beauty –
Who will protect me? God is not deaf to my cries
I am deaf to His in the noise of the Universe that was once
the music of the spheres. I love my Christ, not the Order.
I'm proud not pious, but I love my Lady of Guadalupe
write Her verse upon verse as I crawl on the riverbed of black stones.
I know from my "First Dream" that I am out of my time;
this country is oppressed and will kill me.
The floods come and ruin the grain and my Sisters
mortify themselves while I tend the multitude; the wasting sickness.
The church has burned my books and taken my worldly things.
My stigmata is the sores of these wretched, their crying,
an abyss of darkness that consumes the abyss of light.
Though I don't know if I was ever really here,
I know where I am going.

Poet In Eden

On his visit to America in 1929,
Federico Garcia Lorca left New York City
in summer to visit a friend in Northern
Vermont.

Poet In Eden

Where would Eden be but north
of the City and southwest of the Kingdom?
The map you bought will only do you so much good.
The compass goes crazy inside with the minerals
in these mountains that wash down to the table
to make hard water in the wells.
Lakes and ponds stay cold through August.
The constant sound of rushing water
and the wind in the branches make you
block your ears to drown it out;
The boughs go up and down with a sound of their
own, and you can see the dark places between.
Then know it is mad to go to the country
to rest from the heat of the city.
Wherever you go, there you are.
A special guest
A solitary who finds solitude unbearable,
Worse in the pretence of company.
If the masque of comedy slips
So falls the hero into pastoral tragedy.
Bless you for finding the warm weather
Depressing. Impossible to translate this Eden,
even in letters to your sisters on birch bark
written with the blood of poison berries
under the hanging crape myrtle.
The heavy obligation of the temperate day
To be out of doors or open a window
when all you want to do is stay
in the shade of the parlor and play piano.

This pleases the old women
and the children and you
can make out as long
as you're amusing: They whisper,
"Is he musical?"
"A little odd if not."
So sing for your supper
for if they knew the abyss
of your deep song or sonnets
of dark love you would be
put on the high road
Un Chien Andalou
An untouchable like the
stray black three legged
dog the old men throw
stones at and call
"Nigger."

Only the children can
know the hierarchy of insects,
the veritas of puppet shows and
what the phases of the moon mean.
You would become like them,
follow the sun's circumference.
Reach up and wear it like an amulet,
this burning millstone around
your neck as you
pipe them into the depths,
singing when the water
rushes in and the light
illuminates the lake forever.

Lake Eden

You could never count all its
smaller tributaries, flowing like broken
capillaries to pool a mile wide and a mile deep;
"And a river went out of Eden to water the garden,
and from thence it parted and became four heads..."
More like some serpents you see
around the woman's brow,
lift the slab and fire ants break
out, omen birds turn to dragonflies
and the bullock eating grass is a black eye
like the wood knot in the whorl
of the tree trunk that can't blink
back light breaking up
on the water; everything's in motion
All broken mirrors inverted see nothing
unless the darkness is something.

Eden Mills

The only industry is the asbestos mine.
Water wheel and millstone turning,
They grind the white to powder and they grind
exceedingly fine, still dust on the wheel,
but if they knew then what happens when you take
it into your lungs and years later spit up blood
and fill with fluid, you drown the same as if you
waded into the lake with your pockets full of stones.
Whenever you see
broken branches they are the arrows
in the side of Saint Sebastian.
Three trees on the side of the hill and you see
the three men hung naked to the elements;
two criminals and the Man God, heads down
die of thirst before the floor is swept clean
and boys burn the mill down on Halloween.

Lower Eden Falls

When you can't go any lower and the sunlight
strikes you hair of jet and brilliantine you notice
one of the notches between even higher land
and the last ditch. The man two paces behind you
tells you in his measured Spanish (better than your
broken English) that it is called "The Devil's Gap."
You have to turn back at this point if you want
to get home before dark. His home; yours is an ocean
and an Old World away so you walk out knowing
what you're leaving, sweat on your brow, everything
hurts, and a branch snaps back to tear your eye.
You would like to fall down on the ground
and play dead like you did when you were a kid.
Cry like your mother did when she knew you would never
marry or give her a son. Hunters' guns in Echo Valley
answer back and you smell powder, tongue tastes metallic.
This wilderness, cemetery, and orchard is no place
for you to overstay your welcome.
Nobody had to give you the word.
Your shadow is up and gone
Leaving is the better part.
You are Southbound
Sailing to another
America.

HYPERDULIA

Hero: One Hero died defiled; but I do live,
      And surely as I live, I am a maid.
                      Much Ado About Nothing

Anna Sophia

She was meant to be an angel.
Something over the earth, not of it.
Apparitional. Both the shadow and the glow
Of one white candle that throws no heat
Shining only on itself, the hard finish
On a cold pearl.

She always kept to herself.
Left her days idle but for wreathing flowers &
Naming the birds by their singing.
Her silent footfall around the slivered smile
Of the sundial counts the hours.

She made midnight bright as noonday,
For her the moon would hold its yolk --
The stars bequeath a diadem
Where she holds sway among grass
Long alight with fireflies, like a field full
Of fallen sky.

She has her way with you
Her face behind the veil half hidden
Fables a life for you from thin air,
A curious story with no beginning, no end
No middle. You've already
forgotten it by the seal of the print
Of her lip.

Kneel down and try to bind her feet
Cleave to her waist like a sheaf of wheat
Tie on her sash and go with the grain
Sift and scatter the seed as the birds
Lift and carry off one white rib of her hair

Last night I slept and saw
A cloud of fire coming through the hay.
It was the vision that put flesh on her bones,
The drum of her name's incantation
That made her come and made her dance away.
This is all my fault, through my fault,
my most grievous fault. She said,
  "Look to the light but don't ever love me."

All Things Said And Left Unsaid

I

All things said and left unsaid
I kept in a closed book and a sealed vessel.
She gave me the corn tassel from a stalk
of Silver Queen and I gave her the yellow apple.
She took and split it open to try and find
the diamond, then ate skin and flesh, core and seed.
For me she saved the sharp stem
put it out in my open hand,
closed the red petals of her hard nails
to blossom in my palm.
She turned to face me with eyes full
of Sun, smiling a mouth of blonde diamonds,
Telling me my fortune: "The only Rose without
thorns will be your marriage."

II

I wrote her of the coming of the summer eclipse.
She saw it, but I didn't, fretting alone under
a clouded sky, the lunar transition opaqued
to my eye. Would that we had watched together
on a high hill, though my Sovereign doesn't thrill
to see a Lady-in-Waiting hide her face in her hands.
Fitting to part over the bridge on the river.
Not much music on the humid air but the dull
chant of rowers below the falling tresses
of her loosened hair.
She is cool enough,
though frozen confection melts on her lips,
words wound though the sound is soft,
sting of a kiss in the ear while the calloused hand
feels the burn beneath the soft slip
when we lean to see no reflection
from the brown water by the broken reeds.
She's leaving. I'll be gone and forgotten
before the first snow this winter.

III

This tree has bloomed and grown to fill
the contours of your absence,
silvered tracery on the slender bodice.
White blossoms from the wreathed branches
flake down like first snow and moths
flit around the top to spin a crown
of leaves and cloudberries, like flowers
themselves in flight. There are harps and lyres
enough already, hanging in the air
weighing down the boughs with tribute,
I, too, a willing witness to be proven
on the tree, though a self-made martyr
is a lesser thing. Soft, a feminine ending.
O nail my heart to love thee.

Acknowledgements: Some of these poems appeared in the following journals:
Bennington Review: "Eventide," "She Herself," White Magick;"
Blue Railroad: "Tell All, Ann Dvorak," "I Tried to Die But Now I Want To Live- Jennifer Jones";
Dark Stardust: "The Seer," "Anna Gaia;"
Gandy Dancer: "Her Leaving, Her Wedding, Her Keening;"
HOLDOUT: "The Quarry," "Down The Cape," "Rose Window/Venus Rising"

Front cover photograph: Cynthia, Moon Goddess, Boston Studio Photography
No date, anonymous. Author's collection.
Back cover photograph: The Delli Colli Madonna
Author's collection.

Sean Andrew Heaney received his Masters Degree in Poetry from Bennington College on the Jane Kenyon scholarship. He wrote a weekly Poetry column for the Boston Herald and worked on Special Collections at The Boston Public Library. He was librarian at The Boston Ballet School For Dance Education, and has given poetry readings all over New England, New York City & Los Angeles. He was a guest poet at The Vermont Studio Center in Johnson, Vermont. A Vermont native, he now lives in the Northeast Kingdom of Vermont.